BUSINESS-DRIVEN
COMMUNICATIONS

Setting a Higher Standard
to Reach Target Audiences,
Grow Revenue and Capture
New Markets

LEIGH ANN SCHMIDT

Printed in the United States of America

First Printing, December 2013

ISBN-13: 978-1494371029
ISBN-10: 1494371022

Incisive Publishing
P.O. Box 270246
Austin, TX 78727
www.incisivecommunication.com

CONTENTS

Foreword

by Darryl K. Taft

Longtime technology reporter,
Currently at *eWEEK*

She's the real deal. Spend five minutes with Leigh Ann Schmidt and you'll know what I mean. As a reporter, I deal with dozens of PR reps every week. Many of them are your average company mouthpiece with a script full of marketing buzzwords. And then there are the ones I enjoy working with because I know our time spent together will be productive and will likely result in a solid news story.

Since we started working together more than 15 years ago, Leigh Ann has consistently been one of those "ones." She's honest, reliable, business-minded, wise, thorough...not to mention, funny. She's always been a valuable resource to me and the organizations she's worked for, but now with this book and through her consulting work, she's helping all types of companies understand the business value of communications and how to refine their approach to achieve communications excellence.

There are plenty of books written by journalists and PR people alike that focus on the practice of public relations, tactics and new vehicles of communication. If Leigh Ann ever writes one those books, every PR person should probably buy it. But it's her business-driven approach to communications and her experience making communications a driver of profitable growth for Fortune 50 companies that makes this book a must-read for CEOs.

I think there are a lot of good PR people out there, but I think that business expectations and marketing-led communications efforts don't always allow those good PR people to do their best work. I've been writing about businesses and their technologies long enough to have seen their PR people come and go a few times over. As the people change, what an organization considers news and how it approaches announcements and reporter engagements stays the same. Corporate processes do influence the type of press releases and emails that arrive in my inbox, and PR people can only be as good as their organizations allow them to be.

Some organizations have impressive communications programs, but most could be doing so much better...and this book is a good first step in how to get there. On a personal note, I'm proud of Leigh Ann. Never one to settle for mediocrity, she always wants to make things better. Once she learns something, she wants to teach it and share her knowledge with others so they too can benefit. As long as I've known her, she's never been someone to take the glory. Rather, she's happy to give others credit as long as good work is being done...a rare find anywhere in business today.

"Business-Driven Communications" is a quick read that gets to the heart of the problems corporations face with their traditional communications practices and how they can be remedied. Throughout, Leigh Ann follows her own advice and makes her message simple, direct and to the point. She wants every company to be great at PR. I hope that after you're finished reading, you will be inspired to improve the way you approach corporate communications. Not only will it help your bottom line, but journalists around the world will thank you.

Chapter One

CORPORATE PUBLIC RELATIONS IS DEAD

Corporate public relations is dead. That is, if you are to believe Wayne Burns, the director of the Center for Corporate Public Affairs. In a July 8, 2013 article in O'Dwyers (1), Burns said:

> PR *"is dead as a strategic management function in large organizations and corporations, its original intent and utility surviving only on the tactical fringes of marketing communications areas within corporations."*

> PR has long been *"on life support, its utility and usefulness for most corporations as a core management function has been terminal since the late 1990s: in the 21st Century, **its outcomes more readily align with marketing communications objectives than those of the corporate***

public affairs functions managed in most companies."

In the same article, *New York Times* columnist David Carr was also quoted as saying, "Corporate PR heads mostly hide behind 'underlings' who deliver 'slop.' Almost all PR heads are hidden from view. Not even their names are available on company websites and definitely not their direct phones or emails."

These sentiments aren't those of lone voices in an otherwise flourishing arena. Based on more than 20 years of first-hand experience, I also believe that corporate PR - at least as a strategic driver for a business – is "dead" because of the mismanagement of the function in-house, an over-reliance on outside PR agencies, and an increasing gap between business knowledge and functional output.

Corporate PR today tends to align to product marketing and sales objectives rather than business priorities. Smaller companies, or those just getting started (with fewer than 50 employees), will not usually have budget for both a marketing and a PR lead. To get the most "bang for their buck," companies initially hire the marketing person because of their focus on sales support and pipeline, and then have them manage the PR budget and agency support (which, at its most basic level, is issuing informational press releases).

It's not an ideal situation, but one that makes sense when operating on a small scale and trying to grow. The company might not be getting legitimate or consistent press coverage, but the press release on the internet is something to point to. And hey – some noise is better than no noise as you are starting out, right? But as a company grows, so does its sphere of influence and ability to expand and increase annual revenue. Unfortunately, many business practices and processes established early on don't grow and evolve with the business – companies just add more bodies to do the work. As the business grows, the PR manager and team get hired, but they are still reporting to the head of marketing with marketing ultimately controlling PR.

Now there are just more people doing things "the way we've always done it."

Organizations around the world continually issue press releases that aren't meeting news criteria or generating actual press coverage. Companies remain under the assumption that the issuing of a press release on a wire is "success."

This isn't good PR. There are better ways for businesses to approach communications that can open the channels that let good PR happen. Companies are losing out by not realizing the full potential of the communications teams in their organizations, all while farming out core responsibilities and key reporter relationships to third-party PR agencies.

Imagine if research and development were "dead" and the only value obtained by them was achieved through a third-party vendor? That would be unacceptable because they are your future and the key to your business' sustainability, right? I would argue that corporate communications is just as important. Not only can your communications team influence public perception, but it can drive demand for your future products or services. If communications is as critical to your long-term success as R&D, then it's high time for organizations to raise the expectations of their corporate communications teams and enable them to change the existing bonds of work in order to succeed.

Even if you do have people on your communications teams that are capable of delivering this type of value to your organization, they may not be empowered to succeed. I've worked with a few "dud" PR people in my time, but I've worked with far more brilliant and talented PR people who haven't been tapped for even one-tenth of their potential value.

I've seen brilliant minds who can lead winning press strategies held to the mercies of severely dysfunctional marketing organizations, and I've seen incredible communications leaders repeatedly being tapped to make routine announcements that don't generate actual news coverage. These people can drive and deliver news and media strategies that can help move the needle for the business, but marketing has them otherwise occupied.

Mobility and social media have changed the way people receive information, which has caused turmoil in the world press. While the internet has given more power to the reading audience and allowed customers to have a wider range of news choices, it has also magnificently increased the supply of noise fighting for mind share.

Organizations are becoming more skilled at pushing out information via their own channels, but that isn't enough. A first-party push of information will never be considered proven, reliable or recommended without third-party validation and agreement. With news sources and standards in flux, traditional approaches to corporate public relations and communications range from unpredictable to unsuccessful.

We can change this. It's time to not only bring corporate PR back from the dead, but to elevate the function and enable communications to become a driver of profitable growth. I wrote this book with the CEO in mind, but you don't need an MBA to understand it. My goal is to make it easy for anybody in any business function – in any industry around the world – to understand what it takes to achieve communications excellence.

The good news is, achieving communications excellence is easier and more cost effective than you might expect. All it requires is a shift in approach and the empowerment and training of your teams.

Chapter Two

IS ANYBODY EVEN LISTENING TO YOU?

Let's talk about the news cycle. Do you understand how news gets disseminated? This isn't a trick question. Do you really know? Or do you just know that your PR team issues press releases driven by product marketing teams whose work is aligned to product roadmaps? Let's dig a little deeper.

There are two main press release distribution services: PR Newswire and Business Wire. Both would argue their differences until they are blue in the face, but both are so similar that we can lump them into the "wire" category for our purposes. These wires issue thousands of press releases per day. Companies like yours have contracts with the wires (either directly or through your press agency) where they pay a certain amount of money to issue press releases. Depending on how deep your pockets are, you could issue 10 press releases a day or 10 a year.

It doesn't matter to the wire service, as long as you pay the fee for distribution.

Global and regional news organizations have paid subscriptions to the wires – from the *Associated Press* to the *Greenwood Commonwealth* and all types of trade and industry rags and broadcast stations in between. I know what you're thinking: "Great! I pay to distribute. They pay to receive. As long as my communications or marketing team issues press releases on a wire, people who write about this stuff know what we're doing. Right?" Wrong.

There was a time more than 25 years ago when a press release carried some weight. It was the way news was disseminated by organizations, and reporters went to the wires to pull the day's news. But since the explosion of data on the internet, reporters have not had the luxury of scanning the wires to look for news to write about, interviewing several sources to decode the gibberish in the press release, then pitching it to their editor to see if it is a story they can pursue. It shouldn't be hard to understand that publications that used to employ hundreds of reporters and editors are now dealing with a dozen or fewer reporters who are still expected to cover the news.

Do this simple math: Let's say an average reporter for a well-known industry trade publication writes four articles per week. That's four articles multiplied by a dozen reporters on staff – or 48 articles per week per publication. An average of 3,000 press releases cross the wires every day. Multiply that by five for the days of the work week – bringing an average of 15,000 press releases issued every week. And we haven't even taken into account 'breaking news' that isn't driven by a press release and often trumps any planned news. But if we are looking at press releases alone, yours are among 15,000 competing for 50 coveted spots in your targeted press. That's a bit overwhelming, isn't it? Do you still believe that these reporters are just sitting there waiting for your press release to cross the wire so they have something to write about?

Over time, text becomes easier if it is more like speech
To make it easier for people to understand what your business has to offer, you need to speak a language they understand. As far back as the

1880s, Lucius Adelno Sherman (2) discovered that the English sentence was getting shorter. The average sentence in his times was 23 words in length, as opposed to 50 words per sentence in Elizabethan times. In his findings, Sherman stated:

- Literature is a subject for statistical analysis.
- Shorter sentences and concrete terms help people to make sense of what is written.
- Speech is easier to understand than text.
- Over time, text becomes easier if it is more like speech.

I want to make sure you didn't miss that last part: *Over time, text becomes easier if it is more like speech.* If businesses want people to know what they can do to solve their customers problems, they need to make all public press, marketing and advertising materials easy to read and understand for men, women and children between the ages of nine and 99 – or the group I like to call "Everyman."

I can hear you now: "That might be fine if you're selling soda to customers, but our customers understand our 'techno-speak,' and it's important to highlight our new wiz-bang appliance that now holds 12 terabytes of data vs. the previous five. That's more than double its previous capacity!"

Wrong again, and here's why: you're giving too much credit to the people holding the purse strings in the companies you're selling into. You're assuming that the CEO and people in finance know as much as the IT director to whom you might be selling your "wiz-bang techno awesomeness." You know sales don't happen in a silo. Restrained budgets are drawing on all aspects of an organization from sales to operations, and these are reviewed by those in leadership positions in an ongoing manner. In order for whatever you are selling to become a priority for a business, the CEO, the VP of finance, the VP of operations, the CTO, the director of Human Resources, et al, all need to have a general feeling and understanding about how your solution is going to make their business better or save money by purchasing it.

Of course if it is a wiz-bang techno software solution, it's the CTO's job to ensure it's the best and most complete solution for the intended purpose, and it's her/his job to report and make recommendations in order to obtain the budget for the purchase, installation and training. Beyond the CTO, the senior leadership team doesn't need to know the ins and outs of how Jeremy, the recent Yale grad, is overseeing six full-time and two part-time employees, over the course of 158 total work hours to install, upgrade, integrate and train 67 employees on a new solution that is going to improve call center time by 53 percent.

Do you see how I just wore you down with frivolous and insignificant details to tell you that this new solution for the company **will improve call center response times by 53 percent?** Just like the business leads that don't care for the deep dive outside of their immediate controls, I wore you out before we got to the best part! That is what is happening in business communications – from press releases to marketing materials. Invented techno-speak and marketing babble is complicating the message and clouding the clear and direct customer benefit. And if potential customers and partners don't easily understand how you can benefit them, you lose them.

In order for organizations to influence how their customers feel about them in the press, they must shift the traditional and outdated marketing-led expectations of their media relations and communications teams. When communications is armed with the ability to simplify and align a business' priorities with a message that readers want to hear, that's where you can begin to make an impact.

Chapter Three

THE EVERYMAN PRINCIPLE

To understand the value of simplifying your communications, it's important to understand how news organizations work. Journalists, editors, publishers, writers and bloggers want one thing: readership. Readership equals advertising dollars, which equals jobs, which equals growth.

In order to get and retain readership, they have to write about things the readers care about. Everyone wants to read about things that affect them, both professionally and personally. Telling someone about your new device or what it can do is hardly as effective as showing them how you can help them. People are too busy to look outside of what is causing them heartburn at work, or what is keeping them up at night. Everyone is just trying to get through their day, and unless your message is easy to understand and demonstrates benefit quickly, they will move on because they just don't have time to look deeper.

Journalism 101

Journalists and writers earn readership by consistently providing "need to know" details that interest the reader with balanced and unbiased coverage. Across the world, Journalism 101 begins with teaching students how to write a lead (or "lede," if you prefer). The way they do this is, the teacher dictates a set of facts and the class attempts to write the first paragraph of the news story – or lead.

In my first journalism class, the professor provided these facts for a story to run in the local newspaper:

- *The Texas Department of Public Safety said repairs on the northbound and southbound lanes of the I-35 lower deck will begin Monday.*
- *Exits and on-ramps between MLK Blvd. and First Street will be closed from 6 a.m. – 3 p.m. daily until repairs are complete.*
- *To help prevent gridlock, marked detour signs will be provided to navigate the downtown area.*

- *Repairs expected to be completed by 3 p.m.*
  on Thursday.

When the class turned in our leads, we had all basically written the same thing in various ways: "I-35 exits and on-ramps between MLK and First Street will be closed from 6 a.m. – 3 p.m. beginning on Monday and ending Thursday." We were all wrong. My cantankerous professor screamed, "You all missed the point! The lead is: Leave extra time to get to work next week!"

We did miss the point of the story for the readers. We failed to take into consideration the readers' bottom line. Traffic was going to be really screwed up, and drivers were going to be put out. The details of when, where, how and why would come after the WHAT.

Famed journalist, screenwriter and director Nora Ephron (3) also spoke of a similar experience on her first day of journalism class. Let's see if you can figure out what the lead for her class was. The details her teacher dictated went something like this:

- *Kenneth L. Peters, principal of Beverly Hills High School, announced today that the faculty of the high school will travel to Sacramento on Thursday for a colloquium on new teaching methods.*
- *Speaking there will be anthropologist Margaret Mead, educator Robert Maynard Hutchins, and several others.*

Did you figure out the lead? According to Ms. Ephron's teacher, the story was…

"There will be no school Thursday."

The value of third-party validation vs. pushing out marketing-driven press releases
Now that we've had a little journalism lesson, let's get down to brass tacks. I've already talked about how inundated the wires are with daily press releases. When you're competing with more than 3,000 press releases from all types of industries crossing the wires on a daily basis, you need to understand that the press release is not an effective way to generate news or influence the way people feel about your business. More importantly, and despite what

marketing thinks, a press release does not generate sales.

News that is written by respected third-party publications and read by a large audience of potential customers can and will influence the buying habits of your customers and help generate sales. To put it simply: you can tell me how great you are all day long, but I'm not going to believe it until an unbiased source tells me so, or until I experience it for myself. And the quickest way to get that unbiased source to write about your news is to demonstrate customer value.

Reporters are inundated with phone calls from press reps with whom they have existing relationships, tweets from the companies or customers they follow for their beat, and texts and emails from thousands of press reps pushing their latest version of 'news' down reporters throats. Reporters answer to Managing Editors which report to Editors, all the way up to the Editor in Chief.

The Editor in Chief frequently reviews how many views articles get, establishes editorial calendars for features throughout the year, and works with publishers on relevant ad space and dollars. The more people their news appeals to, the more readers, the more views, and the more advertising dollars. This isn't science, but simple truth: the more relatable your news is, the better chance it has of getting covered in influential publications from the *Associated Press* to *IT Business Edge*.

Apple co-founder Steve Jobs understood this principle, and he was immensely successful for having used simple-to-understand "dumbed-down" language to promote one of the most advanced and integrated hardware, software, and mobile internet solutions to hit the market: the iPhone. At MacWorld San Francisco in 2007 (4), instead of communicating in the language of Apple's traditional target audience, he spoke to every individual in every market around the world – not only to the mobile techno-nerds who were looking to upgrade in the mobile market, but rather the Everyman who could be convinced to buy cutting edge if it were just easy enough to use. Steve Jobs didn't talk about megahertz and gigahertz, but rather used phrases like "edge-to-edge glass," "retina display," and "LED backlighting" to demonstrate value in user experience. The rest, as they say, is history.

Technical details, product specs and design features (all of which are driven and prepared by marketing) can and should always be available on corporate websites or blogs for the nerds that need to know. But in any industry, the nuts and bolts will bore the average reader and always bury the benefits within complicated language.

Chapter Four

IMPROVE YOUR AIM TO HIT YOUR MARK

Here are some examples of organizations that had very good news to announce, but missed their mark and an ever bigger opportunity by using technical industry jargon in headlines for what I consider to be poorly executed news efforts. The following press release headlines (5) were randomly selected from publicly distributed press releases on Business Wire during a quick look at its distribution on August 6, 2013, at 3:09 p.m. ET.

While anybody with access to Google can probably do a search and figure out who these companies are, in an interest of protecting (or at least not bashing) the innocent, I've redacted the company names. Here are the examples:

█████████ Medical Center Chooses CADD®- Solis Ambulatory Infusion System

If you don't work for the IT department at the medical center or for the makers of the CADD-Solis Ambulatory Infusion system, chances are you don't have a clue what this means. Why would you issue this headline that turns off 99.99 percent of your potential audience? Instead, a headline like █████████ *Medical Center to Use New Portable Pain Management Systems to Reduce Length of Stay and Increase Patient Mobility* could tell Everyman what it does and how it helps patients.

As a citizen, you would read this and understand that advancements are being made in medical care at the medical center, and you are likely to think of them if you have a choice for a future hospital stay or procedure. As a member of the Board of Directors for Massachusetts General Hospital, this might catch your attention to see how your facility could benefit from using a similar system. If you are a shareholder in a medical software technology firm, you might read this to see what the competition is selling.

Are you catching my drift? The techno speak (CADD-Solis Ambulatory Infusion System) only means something to people who know what it is to begin with. And all of the effort and money it took to issue the press release only resulted in coverage in *two* online publications: The Minneapolis Star Tribune and The Herald Online (both hometown publications for the system maker).

The company should have saved the minimum three weeks it took them to draft, re-write and finalize a press release that nobody saw or cared about. They could have saved the several hundred dollars it cost to issue the press release and instead contacted the two hometown publications directly, provided them with a press release that could be found on the company's webpage for further details, and called it a day for this lackluster approach to disseminating the news.

Please understand that what you see here with this press release is not unlike what is going on in good companies around the world, and likely your very own organization. I'm not here to simply point out pointless communications, but provide you with effective and probably cheaper communications examples to help you grow your business through integrated and effective communications.

I'm giving you examples of poor communications and the seemingly ingrained *need* of organizations to outdo one another with technical jargon to sound *unique*, but only so that I can prove to you the value of changing your approach to your organization's communications.

Overuse of industry jargon isn't just a problem in the world of software and technology. Take this next example I found on the wire:

████████'s Breakthrough Algal Protein Launches as Key Ingredient in New Twinlab® CleanSeries™ Veggie Protein Powder

Again, you would have to work for the company or be a current consumer of their Veggie Protein Powder to be able to decode the value that a new breakthrough algal protein brings when it will be available in the upcoming CleanSeries version.

Instead, a headline like ████████ *'s New Algal Protein Gives Athletes a "Clean" Supplement That Doesn't Sacrifice Performance* would be better understood by the general public, which includes athletes, trainers, parents, sponsors, etc. etc…

According to the Nutritional Business Journal, the Vitamins, Minerals and Supplements (VMS) industry is projected to top $60 billion in 2021. This is a huge market with a variety of Everyman players, but few of them will appreciate such a narrow message. By simplifying the message, people who take supplements would now know there is a new natural protein they can use to maximize their performance. Trainers and physical therapists for athletes from middle-school to Olympic teams (and every local corner gym in between) can read and comprehend that there is a new natural protein available. When Everyman understands the point and the benefit to customers, targeted selling to specific accounts and customers only becomes easier.

From a quick Google news search, I see this press release was picked up by MarketWatch – a bit better than the local press that the medical center software solution received because it is a sight visited by investors. But with a further Google search of the company, I also learned that they are using this algal protein to create a 'cleaner fuel' for skincare products available at Sephora. Holy communications goldmine, Batman! This is the kind of stuff that can and should be understood by everyone, and is a name understood and coveted by press - but for some reason the company is still using hyped up lingo and product jargon in misguided and expensive press releases.

Here is one final press release example from the construction industry. This press release used two meaningless and superfluous adjectives to make their construction projects sound important instead of speaking to their potential value to residents – where the real value and prestige (by way of paid monthly rent) is earned.

████████ Begins Construction on Two Prominent Developments on Renowned Sunset Strip in West Hollywood

This headline does not explain the value of *prominent* developments in the *renowned* location. You would have to be in L.A.-based construction or real-estate to decode the meaning of prominent and renowned in this specific market.

The headline has one chance to get the attention of the reader. If this company had used simple language that spoke to customer value, they could have reached not only construction and real-estate colleagues, but also shareholders, future occupants, parents or trustees of future occupants, as well as potential new retail outlets that would further drive up the market value in the area. A more simple but explanatory headline like *New* ███████ *Properties are Within Walking Distance of Shopping, Dining and Entertainment Amenities on Sunset Strip in West Hollywood* could have better reached Everyman.

It's easy to point the finger at the press rep whose name is on the press release, but based on traditional organizational structures, it's likely a director or VP of marketing, a president or the CEO himself who needs to take a large part of the blame. If your press rep has to sacrifice clarity in company press materials because higher-ups demand marketing jargon to ensure key messages, programs or platforms are included, they can't be of much help to you.

Step away from the marketing jargon

When reporters see overused marketing "blah blah blah," words, their eyes glaze over, their ears tune out, and they immediately begin regretting their belief that this piece of news might be different. If you want to get a reporter's attention (and dare I say, respect), your organization should avoid using these popular marketing terms when pitching news, speaking to reporters, or writing press releases:

- Optimized
- Unique
- One-of-a-kind
- Best-in-class
- Best-of-breed
- Revolutionary
- Strategic (especially strategic partnerships)
- Leader/leading/leading provider
- Solution
- Proactive
- Innovative/innovator/innovation
- Award winning
- Cutting edge

- Breakthrough
- Value proposition
- Bleeding edge/cutting edge
- Ecosystem (unless you are actually talking about a biology community of interacting organisms and their physical environment)
- Any superfluous adjective that doesn't itself describe what you mean when you use it: best, top, great, exclusive, premier, fastest, dynamic, biggest, amazing, legendary, groundbreaking, iconic, win-win (the 90's called, they want their term back), and mission critical.

You have to be able to get reporters' attention quickly and effectively, or you lose them. There's nothing like a *super duper awesome headline and bleeding edge press announcement about your strategic leadership* to really put them off.

Chapter Five

MAKE YOUR "NEWS" NEWSWORTHY

Of course, there's more to it than crafting a great headline and making your news relevant to Everyman. If your press releases aren't generating press coverage, chances are the information they contain isn't considered newsworthy outside of your company. Here are common things organizations regularly announce in press releases that are rarely (if ever) reported in the news:

Awards or favorable analyst reports
Reporters will not write articles about an award you have won (especially after the awarding organization already announced who won), nor will they write a story about a positive analyst report or magic quadrant you are in. These are great speaking points/supporting messages that help demonstrate industry leadership when pitching actual news to reporters, but

awards and analyst reports do not make the news.

Version 2.5.6 of your product
Product upgrades that now do what you said they were going to do don't pass news muster. Unless there is something totally new and totally different about what the product was already doing for customers, it's not news. If it's that new and different, it should probably be a new product anyway.

Changes in executive leadership or management
Unless you are announcing a new CEO or president, nobody cares about who is moving up the ranks of your organization. That is expected. Reporters want to write about who is leaving your organization and why – and I hope you know that you never want to announce that. It is a best practice not to comment on changes in organizational leadership unless, if by doing so, it alleviates customer concern. For example, if your organization has been flailing due to lack of leadership, you might announce that you've hired someone to fix the crisis and get the

company back on track. All other executive pats on the back need to be saved for the About Us section of your website.

Partnerships

Reporters and customers expect that you are forging business partnerships regularly in order to improve the products and services you provide to customers. That's not news; it's business as usual. So unless the partnership will allow your organization to target a new set of customers or position your organization to grab the lion's share of a market, nobody cares. (Of course, sometimes public companies must announce multi-million or multi-billion partnerships that are material to shareholder interests because of the financial implications they have on an organization, but that's not what I'm talking about here.)

Any 'news' coming out of your organization should clearly speak to customer value and how the business is focused on improving the lives, jobs, experiences, etc. of customers. The simple issuing of a press release does not make it newsworthy because you said so.

What reporters want

Reporters get about as excited about press releases as they do annual colorectal exams. Because reporters know that press releases are one-sided corporate speak about something they don't likely consider news, the press release means very little to them.

What does mean something to reporters is:

- News that other reporters or news organizations don't have (an exclusive)
- An angle to the news that other reporters or news organizations don't have (an exclusive angle)
- Customer or other third party who will speak about the news in terms of customer or market value
- Access to the people in the organization who can make sense of the news and provide quotable quotes (researchers, developers, product designers)

- Access to organizational leaders. (Speaking to PR people and reading press releases doesn't cut it.)
- Video, graphics or photos that provide a compelling visual element to the news.

The last thing a reporter wants to hear is, "Today so-and-so announced..." Reporters want to hear, "Next week (or tomorrow) so-and-so is going to announce XYZ. Are you interested in receiving more information under embargo?" (Embargo means reporter agrees to not publish anything about your news until a mutually agreed upon date/time).

Reporters don't get an exclusive feel when they are handed a press release. A good PR agent will know what the reporter wants to hear about, and pick the phone up to pitch them the story. If the reporter wants to know more, the PR agent should then be sending them a pitch (an overview of the story demonstrating why readers should care).

If the reporter wants the story, they will ask to speak to someone in your company to get an overview of the news and answer reporter questions. At that time, the press agent should tell the reporter what visual aids they have to accompany the news, and offer to allow them to see the press release (if there is one) under an agreed-upon embargo. The press release is then used by the reporter as something to reference for product names, any dates or correct spelling of spokesperson names, etc.

The press release should be the "epilogue" to the story. The wrap up that says, "This happened." With the exception of quarterly and annual earnings reports, mergers, and acquisitions (the types of things the SEC mandates are announced to everyone at the same time), press releases should never lead organizations' news campaigns.

If you want reporters to pay attention, make sure you're actually talking to them about news their readers should care about. On the next page is a little litmus test for your organization to take before moving forward with news. If you can't answer these questions, or can't provide answers without using the marketing terminology I listed earlier, chances are – nobody's going to care about your news.

News litmus test

In order for what you want to announce to be considered newsworthy, you need to be able to answer these 10 questions:

1) What is the significance of the new product/strategy/service/initiative you want to announce? (Why should people outside of your organization care about it?)

2) How does it allow your customers to do something they couldn't do before?

3) Who is the target customer/audience for your news?

4) What specific customer problems or pain points does your news address?

5) Are you announcing something that is better than what the competition offers? (Provide quantifiable information about how it gives you an edge over the competition)

6) How do you perceive the marketplace positioning for it?

7) Will it help you gain market share, mind share or grow revenue?

8) Does your news have anything to do with larger global initiatives reported in

the news? (Examples: Green, crime prevention, travel, health, etc.)

9) Can you explain how your news aligns to your organization's business priorities and strategy?

10) What headline(s) do you imagine with your news?

If your organization can answer these questions, then you have armed your communications team with the ability to tell different customer value stories to reporters from business press, to trade press and industry verticals. All they have to do is pick up the phone and send a few emails to get press coverage. A press release doesn't seem so powerful now, does it?

Chapter Six

EMPOWERED PUBLIC RELATIONS

If the members of your press team are worth their salt, they will be aligned with your business leaders and have a functional (if sometimes difficult) relationship with marketing. If your press team is enabled, supported by, reports to, is measured and financially incented by marketing – therein lies a major hurdle that your business needs to clear in order to simplify your message and expand your company's reach. Allow me to explain.

In business school, you learned:

- Sales and Marketing achieve targets linked to developing new markets or increasing sales.
- Human Resources is responsible for recruiting, staff training activities and supporting professional development of staff.

- Finance monitors and supports goals and objectives designed to keep costs low to improve business profitability.
- Production sets targets relating to quality or meeting planned production schedules.
- Information Technology (in the last 20 years) helps organizations improve functional operations and control costs with seamless and integrated IT business solutions.

Where in this list is communications discussed? It's not, but as you know, it most often resides as a subset of the marketing function. A 2012 survey (6) conducted by the Association of National Advertisers aimed at chief marketing officers found that the value public relations delivers as part of the overall marketing mix is increasing for a few reasons:

- Public Relations is closer to the perspectives, objectives and concerns of corporate CEOs than any other communication or marketing discipline.
- Public Relations sees "the whole corporate picture" as it relates to issues that CEOs worry about.

- Public Relations is a key driver of business outcomes critical to organizational success, including crisis mitigation, reputation and brand building, consumer engagement, sales generation, wealth creation, issues management and beneficial shifts in constituent attitudes and behaviors.

What is good PR?

Your corporate public relations team should be the voice and spirit that communicates your strategy to the public. Public Relations is about affecting the way people think and feel about your organization. It really is the "feel good" part of your business. I'm not talking about fluff pieces chronicling do-gooder executives on the rise. I'm talking about articulating *why* people should want to do business with you with news that demonstrates customer value, leadership, research and innovation, and even examples of corporate character.

Don't confuse public relations with advertising and marketing. While the three practices use different approaches to create brand awareness, advertising and marketing are known to spend significant dollars to gets ads or attention to convince you to buy their product. Because public relations influences the audience through a third-party endorsement in the press (which, in turn, puts your news into perspective and gives your business, product or service credibility), the approach must be more skilled and subtle.

Public relations is not about being another way to push marketing materials to press and influencers that also double as customer hand-outs for sales reps, but I can't tell you how many times in my career I have heard a marketing lead demand a press release because it is something the sales people can take into accounts. The marketing team is directly aligned to sales, as they should be. Their job is to provide materials to and enable sales to penetrate, sell into, or grow customer accounts. Marketing might align to the *why* of public relations and advertising, but their focus is on *how* to help sales.

When traditional organizational structures bury public relations communications within the marketing function, it's difficult to gain sustainable traction in the press. When approached correctly, corporate communications and public relations can not only influence the way people feel about your company, but also be a business enabler for profitable growth.

Media and public relations managers have ongoing working relationships with your organization's top executives. Not only are your business leaders in the know about the business' priorities, but they regularly give your elevator pitch to your top customers, investors, analysts, shareholders, and your own employees. Your media relations team has a front-row seat to your vision for the business, and you could be harnessing their knowledge for great gains.

The PR Manager or Director is already in your weekly staff meetings to better understand the state of your business to develop your messages and drive positive press stories about your organization. (Note: if they're not, you're even further behind the curve than most, and you should immediately ask your assistant to send them an invite to future meetings). Why then, do you have them buried under a VP of Marketing and aligned to product roadmaps and working day-to-day with marketing coordinators who have never even met an exec, let alone held a conversation with one? Why aren't you using their knowledge and experience to be a beacon in the market that can help impact all functional areas of your business, including marketing?

Marketing isn't focused on public relations and communications

When I say that Public Relations *should* have a functional, but difficult relationship with marketing, it is because if you want public relations to be your beacon, they have to be enabled to break the old bad habits of marketing when it comes to press releases and success measurement. On average, large organizations have 20 marketing employees per 1 public relations employee. Most of those 20 marketing employees have never had a meeting with or engaged any member of the senior leadership team. Yet, these 20 marketing people push, hound, expect, force and escalate their own marketing plans, programs and agendas that are designed for sales situations, not influencing press and influencers.

As expected, sales and marketing teams create sales materials, lead generation opportunities and trade shows, as well as help get product to customers. Marketing's role is extremely important, but its functional role and strength is not in public relations and communications. I will also argue that marketing must be simplified as well, but that's its own hairy beast that I will tackle in a future publication.

Bottom line, in its traditional sense, marketing is huge and not skilled or focused on media, press and public relations. To have communications aligned underneath the marketing umbrella is a disservice to the unique position they should be in to help lead your organization.

It's time to initiate a separation of church and state between marketing and communications. I say separation of church and state because while the two functions should be aligned under the broader goals of the business, each has its own constituency and methods for reaching them.

In order for communications to align to business strategy in order to execute effective strategy targeting reporters and influencers, they cannot be held accountable to marketing whose audiences are sales and customers. This conflict of interest will continue to see the business delivering product-level storylines that don't speak to business strategy, while continuing to drown in the noise.

I'm not proposing that communications disregard marketing. Obviously the communications team would be fools to not support significant product launches that would get media attention for your organization, and marketing should continue to be a valuable resource to communications. Marketing has inside knowledge of what products and services are being sold to customers in certain industries. They support existing customers, influence future sales opportunities, as well as lead upcoming product launches – many of which should have a media campaign as part of the larger integrated marketing plan.

Under a separation of church and state, marketing can't tell communications what is newsworthy, and communications should engage marketing where it makes sense to support product or program efforts with the press.

So if communications and marketing become separate functions, to whom are they going to answer? The CEO. In the same way the top marketing executive reports to the leader of the business, there should be a top communications executive doing the same. In order for communications to undergo such a radical shift, it is imperative that it become a standalone function. The customary marketing budget that has been used to support communications needs to continue, but the budget needs to be owned, operated and managed by your communications executive, for communications purposes, with no strings attached to marketing.

In time, once your organization's culture and approach to communications and marketing has positively changed, you can achieve even greater success by initiating an integrated marketing and communications function with both groups working more closely together but on equal footing. But we need to learn to walk before we run. In order to come back together with a new understanding and way of working together, a separation of the two functions is necessary to break the existing ties that bind and keep the organization from achieving communications excellence.

While at IBM, I was part of a communications initiative that was born out of the company's corporate transformation. In an effort to close the gap between the CEO's vision and the team of voices speaking on behalf of the company, corporate communications became a stand-alone function working alongside marketing but answering directly to president and chief executive officer Sam Palmisano. On its own, IBM communications aligned the function, team members and tactics to the business' priorities instead of product lines, marketing categories or brands throughout the larger organization...and the results were remarkable.

Chapter Seven

SIMPLIFYLING IBM & NASA AND AFFECTING STOCK PRICE

Back in January of 2007, I had an experience that rarely happens in public relations. I was able to directly tie the work we did in announcing an IBM technology implementation to bolstering IBM's stock price and position. Let me explain.

There are parts of IBM Software that are very technical, but can be relatable to the average consumer. Take Lotus and WebSphere, for example. While the names might not scream *consumer*, their email, chat, and ecommerce abilities can be discussed in Everyman terms because the subject matter is relatable to the types of things Everyman uses at work and home.

In 2006 and 2007, I was managing public relations for one of the most technical parts of IBM Software – Rational. Rational software and tools are used by developers to make developing software and software systems easier. In short, the average consumer doesn't understand Rational software or even need to. But Rational software was being used by developers to create some of the coolest and most cutting-edge technologies in our world. It was time to have Rational be seen not only as a lynchpin of IBM's core software business, but as a driver of tomorrow's technologies that would help IBM and its customers grow.

By this stage, I was already working under IBM communications' new model of reporting – aligning to marketing, but reporting as a stand-alone function to the Chairman of IBM. I was not sitting in weekly marketing meetings, but instead was looking for stories within my part of the business that tied directly into the company's key initiatives. I was having lunch with researchers, IBM Fellows, sales directors and product development managers. I was having conversations with colleagues, finding out what they were working on, what cool things they were involved in, and seeking the types of stories that were going to make IBM Rational not just palatable, but consumable to Everyman.

During this time, I met Swati Moran. She was the marketing manager for Aerospace & Defense Systems at IBM. (I mention Swati by name because if I've learned anything in my career, it is to never miss a chance to sing the praises of those who helped you achieve great results.)

As we spoke, Swati told me that a little-known product she was overseeing was actually being used by the people developing the systems for the James Webb Space Telescope, the replacement for the Hubble Telescope. She went on to say that the business wasn't focused on it and there wasn't budget to do marketing activities around it because the software technology being used for the solution didn't align to the Rational 2007 roadmap and sales pipeline. It wasn't a product that was being discontinued, but it wasn't in the list of products aligned to the group's priorities and go-to-market strategy.

I immediately began seeing headlines for IBM and NASA. It didn't surprise me that the marketing team wasn't burning up my phone about the work with NASA because NASA wasn't using a technology that was reflected in the current roadmap. Because their success was measured by helping sell existing products on the roadmap, they didn't see (or weren't incented to see) how talking about the company's immense capabilities would help them sell their existing roadmap, regardless of what product was being discussed.

Swati used to sell into government accounts, and she knew what kind of influence a story like this could have. While the marketing team (led by the IBM Rational brand/business) may have overlooked this opportunity, we were empowered through our new organizational structure and mission to make critical and strategic communications decisions. I was able to create a communications plan that didn't require 25 marketing people, 10 meetings, 38 fights, six escalations through the management chain, and a go-round with the naming and branding watchdogs just to tell the story.

It was our mission to help the world understand the types of really cool things that were happening because of some IBM Software that most people had never even heard of before. I set a communications plan and crafted a story that spoke to the end result/value of IBM and NASA working together and what it means for "customers" (all of civilization, in this case, as well as software developers and the companies they work for). Our PR team developed and executed a media plan that had different angles for different types of reporters. We set up interviews, followed through with fact-checking, and provided analysts and third-party influencers to reporters we had pitched to validate the stories. Before the press release was put on the wire, press coverage was imminent. When the press release was issued, it was simply the "epilogue" to the bigger body of work. The flag planted on the moon, so to speak. The proof that what we said happened had actually happened.

Here is the first part of the press release we issued. Take a look at the language I used in writing the release to describe probably one of the most technical systems development tools and how it was being used to create an even more technically advanced space telescope (7)…

NASA EYES OPEN STANDARD SOFTWARE FOR NEXT-GENERATION JAMES WEBB SPACE TELESCOPE

ARMONK, NY - 19 Jan 2007: IBM (NYSE: IBM) today announced the National Aeronautics and Space Administration (NASA) is using IBM software to develop the software and systems that will operate the James Webb Space Telescope. The Next Generation Telescope which will succeed the Hubble Space Telescope will look much closer to the beginning of time and hunt for the unobserved formation of the first galaxies.

The Telescope, expected to be launched by 2013, will study galaxy, star and planet formation in the Universe. In order to study how the very first stars and galaxies formed in the early Universe, NASA will look 'back in time' and deep into space using light time *to travel from the present to the past. To study the earliest star formation in the Universe, NASA will observe infrared light, using special instruments optimized to capture this part of the spectrum.*

Nearly 20 years ago when the components and instruments on the Hubble Telescope were developed, software was built by multiple organizations using proprietary software for systems development. This approach meant that maintenance, changes and fixes to components and instruments made required multiple tools. Over the life of the mission HST developed software tools to resolve most of these issues.

Because separate space agencies from several different countries around the world are developing the software that will operate the Telescope's Guidance, Navigation and Control (GNC) systems, Command and Data Handling (CNDH), and the Integrated Science Instrument Module (ISIM) that houses the four primary instruments on the James Webb Space Telescope, it was critical for NASA to weave a common thread throughout the project that would circumvent expensive and time consuming software issues.

To address this hurdle, NASA mandated that each agency develop their systems using open standards-based software from IBM. The software, called IBM Rational Rose Real-time, is a UML-based visual modeling development software that acts as a blue print for the entire multi-decade project, allowing the developers of the various Telescope systems to "drag and drop" software code directly into the blue print where it is then automatically available across the entire project.

Rational Rose Real-time helps these systems developers write applications faster without compromising quality. The IBM software continually verifies project quality along each step of the development process -- including code generation, testing, debugging and ongoing changes -- so that systems development stays on course and without error. This allows the many space agencies working on the James Webb Space Telescope to be more productive and able to deliver reliable code on time -- meeting broader project requirements and industry compliance regulations. Some of the agencies working on the Telescope are also using IBM Requisite Pro, IBM Rational ClearCase and IBM Rational ClearQuest which allows them to synchronize changes within their globally dispersed project teams resulting in faster innovation.

*The full version press release is available for viewing on the IBM press site.

From the headline to the first two paragraphs of the press release, you'll notice we didn't say anything about the name of the technology, the version of it, the top three marketing messages about the software, or the fact that it is specifically Rational Software from IBM. In the general population, people understand IBM, people understand NASA, and people understand space exploration and telescopes. We wanted to announce this news in a way that was palatable to the general masses, not focus on the technology that would have of possibly garnered two or three original stories in IT publications.

It wasn't until the fifth paragraph that we mentioned the name of the technology, and even still described it in general terms for people to understand. Paragraph six gets into the technical details for the developers reading the story who are looking for that specific information.

We took the same Everyman approach when speaking to reporters. Because the goal was news coverage, not simply issuing a press release, we contacted business, trade, broadcast and regional reporters who covered science and technology. We pitched them the story under embargo. I armed our general manager with easy-to-understand messages for the business press, and I prepared our VP of marketing to speak to broadcast and regional press and provided them with B-roll and photos, and I had the lead developer for our software speak to the tech trades.

We developed three different pitches for the different types of press targets. We put the news into perspective for each of their core audiences, and had the story primed, told, supported and fact-checked before the press release ever hit the wire. The press release crossing the wire served three functions: publicly disseminating the information, lifting of embargoes, and having "proof of news" that allowed reporters to get spokesperson and product names, as well as double-check information received during interviews.

The results are in

The resulting news coverage was immense. More than 100 original and re-printed articles appeared in business press, IT tech trades, scientific journals, blogs, stock tickers and local news stations. For an entire 24-hour news cycle, millions of developers, housewives and all of the business owners, engineers and accountants in between knew that IBM technology was at the heart of the telescope that would replace the Hubble.

But there's more to this story. I told you that this news had a hand in affecting the company's stock price. News coverage like I described above goes very far when third-party companies measure your "share of voice" and whether it was positive, negative or neutral when doing quarterly media research.

Obviously an increase in positive news stories and share of voice can only help validate an organization's reputation and sales potential, but this is black-and-white proof that this type of work can even directly impact an organization's stock.

It was this media campaign that caused the Motley Fool (8), a multimedia financial services company, to name **IBM the Best Tech Stock for 2007**. Here is what the Motley Fool said:

> *On the same day this month that **IBM** (NYSE: IBM) released its solid quarterly earnings and reported an 11% increase in net income, management also announced that it had landed a deal to supply NASA with software to help the space agency build the James Webb Space Telescope -- the successor to the Hubble Space Telescope.*
>
> *Although the terms of the deal weren't released, and I doubt very much that it will account for anything more than a blip on Big Blue's income statement, **it is a perfect example of why I think that IBM is not***

only the best blue chip for 2007 but also the best tech stock of the year.

You see, if IBM can supply the software to operate a massive state-of-the-art telescope that can peer into the depths of the universe and then gather and transmit that data back to NASA, there is good reason to believe that it will also be able to supply software for a variety of complex modeling jobs here on earth.

*For instance, automobile manufacturers such as **Ford** and **General Motors** can use IBM's software to make developments to their products more quickly, and pharmaceutical and biotechnology companies like **Pfizer** (NYSE: PFE) and **Genentech** (NYSE: DNA) could employ it to model the complex molecular interactions necessary to create new drugs or find previously unknown connections between a person's genetic makeup and certain diseases...*

The full report can be found online, but you get the gist. This could have been a very different story – and frankly one not worth telling – had we followed the traditional approach with marketing and focused on product feature/functionality instead of the value to Everyman.

This is an excellent example of the power of public relations, and it had nothing to do with what was going on in marketing, product roadmaps or product upgrades. This wouldn't have been the same story, nor would it have had the same results, if the technology or its speeds and feeds had been the focus of the news. In fact, if public relations had been instructed by the priorities of the marketing organization, it likely wouldn't have happened at all.

This isn't a one-off example either. These days, IBM doesn't lead a press campaign, news story, or issue a press release without making it easy to understand and focused on customer benefit. I personally don't believe the company would have had such a successful transformation and once again become a Wall Street darling from the mid-2000s to today without taking this simplified, yet strategically-focused approach to communications.

Chapter Eight

GET IN TUNE WITH INFLUENCERS

Getting your message out to the public extends beyond the world of press and analysts. You need industry influencers on your side. Let's cut to the chase. If your PR team refers to press and analysts as "influencers," it might be time to re-evaluate what they're bringing to your organization. I can't tell you how many lame attempts I've seen by PR "professionals" and "leaders" to jump on the influencer bandwagon by simply changing the way they refer to their core group of press and analysts.

"Influencer" is *not* the new cool name for reporters and analysts; they help influence your audience. An influencer is a third-party individual who understands the work your organization does and speaks positively about it to customers, shareholders, reporters and analysts. They might include venture capitalists, academics, scientists, political leaders or advocates, authors, renowned bloggers or industry experts.

That said, let's talk about the value of a robust influencer network. Back in 2003, a colleague and I drove an influencer event for IBM customers, reporters and analysts. The Future of Work – a symposium we held in Cambridge, Massachusetts, included a panel of authors, civic leaders from the Commonwealth of Massachusetts, venture capitalists, as well as one IBM developer and researcher who spoke from their unique positions and roles in society about the impact of technology on the way we work. We invited customers and partners, along with business, local and trade press to the event, and it was a resounding success.

We didn't announce anything in relation to this event. We weren't selling anything either. This wasn't a tricky or clever way for IBM to push its agenda under the guise of a symposium. The point was to demonstrate the company alongside the respected industry and academic minds leading the conversation about the future of work and the role technology would play. We were building "street cred" (although IBM probably wouldn't have used that term), and perhaps even laying some of the very early groundwork for IBM's evolution to its Smarter Planet campaign (9).

The results included dozens of news stories and analyst write-ups about the Future of Work and what IBM and other industry and civic leaders were doing to make an impact. More than two dozen sales were directly tied to the event. Customers who might have been on the fence about working with IBM to solve their business collaboration issues saw IBM as capable of solving their problems long term, even if the products available in the short term didn't answer all their needs. Shareholders saw IBM leading an important conversation in the market versus answering a singular need with a simple product. And most importantly, the influencers we engaged with now also knew where IBM was coming from, and could speak about the company in a way that was relatable to their existing audiences.

The value of industry influencers
The symposium is more of a one-stop-shop example of how influencers can help drive the conversations you want to have with your core audiences, but it doesn't take an event for their

influence to make an impact. If you want to strategically influence the conversations in the marketplace, it is critical to engage the people who have respected voices in your targeted industries and markets. This is a very different relationship than the traditionally familiar ones between marketing and the customer or between public relations and the reporter. These individuals hold great influence for both of those target audiences, yet you aren't selling them anything or asking them to stump for you.

Your network of influencers are folks who should be aware of your business priorities and how you can help customers. Since these influencers move in powerful circles and know the decision makers, you want these folks spreading the word on the street through their everyday interactions and conversations.

We've talked about the increasing amounts of noise, and the need to rise above the noise. There's not a lot of noise to compete with on elevator rides, on golf courses, in keynote speeches, in university lecture halls, or at networking dinners. Influencers are having the one-on-one conversations in these intimate and familiar settings that could open the door for sales, partnerships and the ever-elusive "feel-good factor" that you want on the street, walking the halls, and in conversations happening about your business.

The key word here is conversation. People know when they are being talked at, sold to, or advertised to – and there are arguably times and places where this type of interaction is expected, if not welcomed. But when you are trying to influence the way someone thinks and feels about something, a hard approach is the wrong approach.

Each concentrated area of the business should have a list of influencers that are already friendly to your organization, or with whom you want to establish a rapport. PR agencies can be very useful in helping identify people outside of your network that you should reach out to. Even more importantly, the senior members of your team know of and have connections with influencers through boards of directors, associations and other organizations.

Your communications team has far reach across your organization – from the executive leadership team, to researchers, product managers and sales. They have the ability to draw on the whole of your organization to help identify the thinkers and leaders in their target fields and industries. Your communications team should consistently update and expand this list of influencers, and create engagements and opportunities to open the dialogue and understanding between the influencers and your organization.

Chapter Nine

STRATEGIC CORPORATE COMMUNICATIONS & THE ROLE OF THE PR AGENCY

At first glance, this section might strike you as a bit granular, but it is important that you have a basic understanding of the PR agency and corporate PR team roles. This can only help as you make business decisions aimed at achieving greater impact with communications.

While a PR agency might make recommendations and bring certain expertise to the table, your corporate public relations communications team are the ones who should set the communications strategy, programs and campaigns – which the agency team can then extend to the large network of reporters, bloggers and influencers. PR agencies can support your organization's PR team by creating media contact lists, tracking editorial calendars, helping write press releases, contacting reporters, and pitching bylined articles.

The main rule you need to understand about PR agencies is this: They are in a subservient role. Remember: your organization owns the dollars that determine how many people they hire on their team to support your services. If you tell them to write and issue one press release a day for the next 365 days, they are going to say yes because that is guaranteed work and money for their own bottom line. No matter how good, bad, big or small your PR agency is, their main objective is to make the client happy so they can keep their business or earn more of it. Simple as that.

Throughout my career, I've worked with dozens of state & local government, non-profits, start-ups, mid-sized and Fortune 50 companies, their PR executives and their PR agencies. One universal truth I have learned over time is this: The PR agency is only as good as your corporate PR person/team.

If you don't have the depth and expertise of a solid corporate communications program to orchestrate the broader delivery of your media and influencer strategy, your agency cannot act as an effective extension. If your communications leaders frequently complain about their PR agency not delivering, they should instead be holding a mirror up to themselves and their teams and asking why they aren't properly enabling the agency to succeed.

A lame and overplayed practice I have seen employed by weak internal PR managers is blaming the PR agency for lack of news coverage and then switching agencies in an attempt to *fix* the problem. Of course, your organization should occasionally review suppliers to ensure you are getting the best service for the money you pay them, but if your communications team frequently references poor agency performance, trust me when I tell you it's most likely their own fault.

PR agencies – an inside look

Let's take a quick look at what goes on inside agencies to give you more insight into what this all means. The majority of fresh-out-of-school PR hopefuls go to work for agencies as account assistants or account executives because it is a large environment that allows them to learn the tools of the trade within a reporting structure that doesn't allow them to fail. All PR agencies have a structure with titles similar to this:

- **Company Director**
- **Associate Director**
- **Account Director** 10+ yrs. experience
- **Account Manager** 7-10 yrs. experience
- **Senior Account Executive** 5-7 yrs. experience
- **Junior Account Executive** 2-5 yrs. experience
- **Account Assistant** 0-2 yrs. experience

Each level of person at an agency has an hourly billing rate. An account assistant has the lowest hourly rate and it goes up from there. When you have a monthly retainer, the account manager is responsible for assigning monthly hours to the account executives and account assistants based on the retainer amount. Since account assistants and account executives have the cheapest billing rates, the majority of your agency's working hours are billed at these lower levels.

What you need to know is the account manager or director usually has some real experience under their belt. They know a pretty good amount about PR, news and writing, and they usually can quickly understand your business and your media goals and priorities. However, they are but one (expensive) person on your bill, so the people doing the daily and hourly work (drafting press releases, pitching reporters, and pulling media lists) are senior account executives and below.

Agencies are churn-and-burn environments where those who are best at their jobs tend to be hired away. This means the worker bees on your agency team are constantly changing. The people who are executing your media strategy are likely less than 5 years out of college, and have only been on your account for months, rather than years – with account assistants, executives and managers changing frequently.

If the PR agency is like college football, your corporate team should be like the NFL

Let's think about this in terms of Division 1 college football and the NFL. Coaches and recruiters in Div. 1 face the inevitable 5-year rule of play. Every single year approximately a quarter of players age out, graduate or are recruited to the NFL. This means that on average Div. 1 teams are looking to recruit 25 new players every year. These players are thought of in five-year plans, and the team is structured accordingly. No coach wants to put all of his eggs in a senior-heavy BCS Championship team, only to turn around the next year and have a very young and green team of players that causes the team to lose standing. They know it takes time to build the strategy and grow the strengths of the individuals and the collective team, and they can't afford to be losing their top talent every year. Their future success depends on them investing as much in the freshman and sophomores as much as they do the juniors and seniors.

Now, reflecting agency turnover, imagine if these college football teams lost their quarterback and star wide receiver at the end of each season, or worse, had two or three quarterbacks every season. Depending on the individuals, there might be some really beautiful moments on the field, but in general, the lack of time working as a cohesive team under a thought-out strategy would prove fruitless in building the kind of team it takes to win a national title.

This is what's happening in the world of agency-driven public relations for corporations. This model has left companies with the problem of losing their "quarterbacks" frequently. Every time they feel like they are getting two steps ahead of the game, getting a new quarterback up to speed (who won't last more than a year anyway) seems like an endless game of chasing their own tails.

Think of your corporate communications team as the NFL, with your agencies and suppliers acting more in a Div. 1 college role. In the NFL, there are no age or time limitations on players. You have the ability to contract your quarterback and star wide-receiver in-house. You now have your key players who are putting your plays into action within your control. If they are good and you want to keep them, you have the ability to pay them their "staying price" either monetarily or through opportunity, or risk losing them to competitive recruiters. The point is – you at least have some skin in the game. You can play a role in whether they stay or go. You don't have that control of a third-party vendor, bound by separate rules and cultures. Your corporate communications team should have as many quarterbacks and star wide-receivers as possible to lead your corporate strategy initiatives, calling on the agencies as second string to support their efforts.

What type of professional should be leading your corporate communications team?

Now let's talk a bit about the type of communications executive you should have leading your organization's communications function. You'll want to hire a strong and experienced corporate communications leader. Because marketing's heavy hand has been hiring communications people internally for some time, it is possible that you don't even have the type of business quarterbacks that you need on your corporate communications team, let alone a "coach" that knows what to do with them.

Corporate communications executives with long careers working for agencies can wind up providing a great disservice to a business. Because their on-the-job experience and leadership in PR has been winning new business for the agency, keeping clients happy and hiring team members to fill changing client needs, there is a greater tendency for them to focus on these areas of expertise. This can easily wind up with the communications function falling back into a comfortable support role for marketing. You want your corporate communications executive to have experience navigating the corporate landscape and be extremely comfortable having the conversations and making the decisions that impact your business and industry.

Agency teams are invaluable for executing and inventing PR tactics to support your strategies and initiatives. At a leadership level, these aren't the people who have the necessary experience to drive communications programs and teams in alignment with corporate business strategy.

In addition to all of the usual expectations of team and budget management experience, your corporate communications leader should embody these main three characteristics:

1) 15+ years of experience – **mostly corporate** – with some agency experience. Anyone with more than half of their work experience at an agency will tend to have greater strengths in matching dollars to bodies than understanding and driving business strategy (MBA or post-graduate business administration experience preferred)

2) Significant corporate experience working with marketing and executive leadership for the purposes of influencing shareholders, customers, and the public through reporter and analyst engagement

3) Experience using communications as a driver of transformation for an

organization (both through internal and
external communications)

What you should be able to expect from your PR team

We talked about having those quarterbacks and wide-receivers working for your in-house communications team. Members of your corporate PR team should be expected to:

-   Drive comprehensive media campaigns that result in positive news coverage, improved media favorability and substantial internet buzz
-   Deliver your company's elevator pitch (including business strategy and customer value) in 15 seconds or less
-   Understand all areas of the business (finance, R&D, operations, sales & marketing, IT) and how their work across all areas can help grow the business
-   Understand the business' top priorities and the goals and programs in place to meet these objectives
-   Work across the organization to consult the business on the most strategic ways to reach readers, listeners and watchers
-   Engage with key press on a daily basis

- Be brilliant writers who can break down technical jargon into customer and business value
- Engage reporters, bloggers, social media and other external audiences only when they are able to clearly demonstrate news value in the conversation
- Manage the agency support team as an extension of the work they are driving, not expecting the agency to do the work your PR team should be doing

What you should expect from your PR agency

And this brings us to the agency. The agency is your front line talking to the press. You should expect that they:

- Have experience working with clients in your industry
- Have existing and longstanding relationships with business reporters and general interest reporters, as well as those writing for the trade publications
- Are brilliant writers who can break down technical jargon into customer and business value
- Work as an extension of your communications team – operating under clearly defined objectives and expectations

Are you wondering if you already have the right "coach" to lead your newly empowered communications organization? Here's a Top 10 List (in the vein of David Letterman) to consider.

10 Signs Your Corporate Communications Leader is in Over His/Her Head:

#10: When you speak of corporate strategy, they immediately go into event-planning mode. (Note: Good news doesn't require dog and pony shows.)

#9: More than half of their work experience has been on the agency side of PR.

#8: Their idea of rewarding success within their teams is handing out "Care Bears" or other tchotchke type junk (this is classic agency culture behavior).

#7: They complain about the agency underperforming, without realizing they are responsible for their performance.

#6: They treat the executive team like clients and reward them with dinners and gift cards for media performance.

#5:   They treat marketing and whoever holds the purse strings like clients and talk about how they will support, instead of take the lead in, company efforts.

#4   They regularly reference two or three big name reporters that they've held relationships with long before they were in their current role, although these relationships don't seem to equate to consistent press coverage for your organization.

#3:   They immediately roll over and acquiesce to the demands of marketing when escalated. They lack the necessary experience and know-how to make recommendations that could more greatly benefit the organization.

#2:   They "happily" report to the VP of Marketing.

#1:   **Before you read this book, you had only thought of press and media relations as a subset of the marketing function because your head of corporate communications has never been able to articulate the value of strategic corporate communications to you.**

Chapter Ten

THE BUSINESS OF YOUR COMMUNICATIONS

Corporations are consistently looking for ways to bridge the gaps between the CEO's vision and all functional areas of the organization to get the desired customer experience and move the business forward. One rather large chasm that exists in Corporate America is the lack of working business knowledge across the support functions, including public relations and communications.

Outside of finance and operations, the majority of your workforce probably received a college education, but not in a business field. Chances are, you have more engineers, developers, English majors and Liberal Arts majors working throughout your company than actual Whatever College School of Business majors. Yet, cycles churn, deadlines are missed, communications are lame and sales is missing their pipeline in an ongoing game of frustration for you.

What if you could impart some real business knowledge into these support functions so that they can better align their daily work to your business priorities? What if a small financial investment in Josh, your tradeshow videographer, could not only produce entertaining videos that people enjoy but also inherently drive the video content to convey your business' key messages? You've just increased Josh's value to your organization tenfold.

Some of your most seasoned professionals have an inherent understanding of what drives the business because of their years of experience and role in your organization's excellence, but many of them have either become complacent and aren't responding to your message as they once were, or they were laid off in favor of hiring two new college recruits for their same salary. Now you are faced with an even younger, inexperienced, non-business educated workforce. Surely you see that chasm I speak of has only gotten bigger, right?

There are companies like Bottom Line Training and Consulting Inc. (10) who travel all over the world to teach non-business graduates working in corporations from 10-400,000 employees what they need to know and understand about the underpinnings of a business. They call the course the Mini-MBA program. This training helps non-business folks improve and maximize their functional roles to not only adequately support the business, but to be a contributing driver of business growth.

This type of investment in training your PR team can yield high results. Imagine your team of quarterbacks and wide receivers who not only understand how to align their work to your core business priorities, but also understand the functional aspects of the organization and the business drivers that set in motion those priorities. Imagine your PR team approaching communications strategies, plans and tactics from the perspective of "how will this help the business?" Wouldn't it be nice if everyone in your marketing and communications team worked this way?

In business, the knowledge workers have become experts within their specific business function: finance, marketing, communications, sales, etc. But that doesn't mean they can truly express the value their function brings to the business they work for. Remember earlier when I told you there are on average 20 marketing people per one communications employee? Do you recall how we talked about the fact that PR is closer to the perspectives, objectives and concerns of corporate CEOs than any other communication or marketing discipline? I don't want to tell you what to do, but it sure seems like a great first step to enable your communications team to think and operate as business leaders.

Matching up the insight and leadership of the CEO with the mouthpiece of the organization can help you achieve more immediate results. Marketing, finance and sales are al large organizations, but the PR team is relatively small with an important strategic role within your organization. You can educate and enable this team for more immediate business results while you work on the slower and more arduous task of changing the culture and processes within the larger functions. Once PR and communications begin to work this way, their work and influence across your organization can only help lead the change you seek throughout the entire business.

In summary
I know you're busy, so I'm going to wrap this up. Here's the net/net of what you can do to drive greater awareness and empower communications to become a strategic driver of your business:
- Hire a strong and experienced communications leader.
- De-couple communications from marketing and have the head of communications answer directly to the CEO (or whoever is in charge) in the same way the head of marketing and sales reports.
- Allow communications to align its function to corporate strategy and business priorities.
- Support and mandate simplified Everyman language across the business, but especially throughout the communications and customer-facing functions.

- Provide communications consulting training to the business functions and marketing support teams about what news is and how to assist the PR team in achieving communications excellence.
- Provide business consulting training to the communications team to teach them to think about the impact of their work on a business level.
- Enable your communications leader to build a world class communications function in-house, with limited, but targeted, agency support.
- Set and expect measurements of success, and then allow communications to succeed.

News and journalism will continue to evolve along with the internet and access to information, and its future will likely hinge on the sustainability and effectiveness of the new measures of accountability that are established for journalism. But none of it will matter if businesses aren't speaking the language of the people and doing so in ways that help them drive profitable growth and increase mind share.

In order to survive and rise above the noise, the pros have to raise their game. Are you ready to raise yours?

References

(1) Article: Corporate PR is Dead by Jack O'Dwyer for O'Dwyers online, July 08, 2013, http://www.odwyerpr.com/story/public/781/2013-07-08/corporate-pr-is-dead.html

(2) Sherman, Lucius Adelno 1893. *Analytics of literature: A manual for the objective study of English prose and poetry."* Boston: Ginn and Co

(3) Nora Ephron interview with the Academy of Achievement, a Museum of Living History, upon induction in 2007. All rights reserved. Interview available online at http://www.achievement.org/autodoc/page/eph0int-4

(4) Steve Jobs introduces original iPhone – MacWorld SF (2007). Posted on YouTube by EverySteveJobsVideo at http://www.youtube.com/watch?v=t2MOwQ089eQ

(5) Information obtained from three separate press releases publicly disseminated via BusinessWire on Aug. 6, 2013. www.businesswire.com

(6) Survey available through Association of National Advertisers, http://www.ana.net/

(7) IBM Press Release: NASA Eyes Open Standard Software for Next Generation James Webb Space Telescope, January 19, 2007, http://www-

03.ibm.com/press/us/en/pressrelease/20901.
wss

(8) Motley Fool article: The Best Tech Stock for 2007
by Jack Uldrich, January 31, 2007,
http://www.fool.com/investing/general/2007
/01/31/the-best-tech-stock-for-2007-ibm.aspx

(9) IBM Smarter Planet, All Rights Reserved
http://www.ibm.com/smarterplanet/us/en/o
verview/ideas/index.html?csr=caus_smarterpl
anet-
20130809&cm=k&cr=Google&ct=USBRB301&S_
TACT=USBRB301&ck=building_a_smarter_pla
net&cmp=USBRB&mkwid=skmyUvdUp_31237
491950_432t5q28552

(10) Bottom Line Training and Consulting, Inc. &
the Mini-MBA, http://bottomlinenyc.com/

Acknowledgements

Thanks to Mom, Dad, Sister, Brother and Jeff –
Your love is unconditional, and your patience
is inexhaustible. I love you more than the moon
and all the stars.

Special thanks to Bob Timpson, David Buckner,
Darryl Taft & Mariella Krause. Your support is
immeasurable.